Super Cute Paper Piecing

DESIGNS FOR EVERYDAY DELIGHTS

Charise Randell

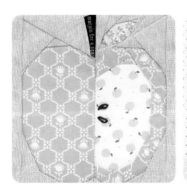

Martingale
Create with Confidence

Super Cute Paper Piecing: Designs for Everyday Delights
© 2017 by Charise Randell

Martingale®
19021 120th Ave. NE, Ste. 102
Bothell, WA 98011-9511 USA
ShopMartingale.com

Printed in China
22 21 20 19 18 17   8 7 6 5 4 3 2 1

**Library of Congress Cataloging-in-Publication Data
is available upon request.**

ISBN: 978-1-60468-879-5

MISSION STATEMENT

We empower makers who use fabric and yarn
to make life more enjoyable.

CREDITS

PUBLISHER AND
CHIEF VISIONARY OFFICER
Jennifer Erbe Keltner

CONTENT DIRECTOR
Karen Costello Soltys

MANAGING EDITOR
Tina Cook

ACQUISITIONS EDITOR
Karen M. Burns

TECHNICAL EDITOR
Debra Finan

COPY EDITOR
Durby Peterson

PRODUCTION MANAGER
Regina Girard

COVER AND
INTERIOR DESIGNER
Adrienne Smitke

PHOTOGRAPHER
Brent Kane

ILLUSTRATOR
Sandy Huffaker

Contents

Introduction

I have loved sewing since I was a little girl. When I was six years old, my mom taught me how to make clothes for my Barbies with scraps of fabric. That time spent learning to sew with my mom ignited a love for sewing that has carried me throughout my life.

When I was 12, for Christmas my dear uncle bought me my first sewing machine, a simple Singer, and I taught myself to make clothing for myself and my family. Home economics sewing was my favorite class in high school, and afterward I had a successful career as a fashion designer. Over the years, sewing has kept me sane and happy and helped me through both the good and challenging times in my life.

A few years back I was lucky enough to discover a vibrant, online sewing community. I joined a few quilting groups online, which introduced me to the technique of foundation paper piecing. It was love at first stitch! Foundation paper piecing allows incredible accuracy when sewing your block together. It looks complicated but is really quite simple.

If you haven't paper pieced before, I will show you how to master the technique by making a simple colored-pencil block. You'll learn how to match seams and fussy-cut motifs. After practicing this technique for years, I have tools that I cannot live without and I'll share them with you. And if you have experience paper piecing, there are lots of more challenging blocks for you to sew! Since I love to make items out my paper-pieced blocks, I have included 10 fun projects. Make yourself a cup of tea, sit back, and enjoy the journey of paper piecing with me. Happy sewing!

~ *Charise*

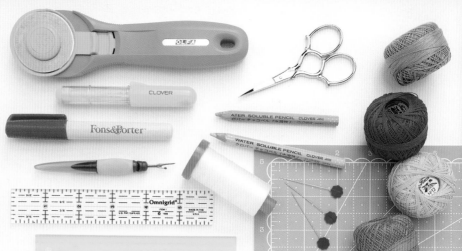

Tools and Techniques

A well-stocked toolbox and basic techniques are essential for quilters. Check this section to see if you have everything you need to complete your projects. Find additional helpful information at ShopMartingale.com/HowtoQuilt.

PAPER-PIECING SUPPLIES

Many of the supplies needed for paper piecing are already in your sewing basket. These are my must-haves for the projects in this book.

Sewing Machine and Specialty Feet. I use my vintage Singer Featherweight for piecing. I use a regular foot for most of my sewing and then switch to a walking foot when sewing over bulky layers. Any standard sewing machine will work well for paper piecing.

Iron. It's important to iron each seam after sewing to ensure a crisp, accurate block.

Scissors. Good quality scissors are essential. I use Gingher dressmaking shears for cutting fabrics and a pair of small embroidery scissors for clipping threads.

Rotary Cutter and Self-Healing Mat. For cutting, I use a self-healing mat and a 45 mm Olfa rotary cutter.

Acrylic Ruler or Add-A-Quarter Ruler. Add-A-Quarter rulers have a ¼" lip that makes it easy to add a ¼" seam allowance around the pattern.

Quilting Rulers. I use a variety of sizes. For the projects in this book, I recommend a 9½"-square ruler for squaring blocks.

Starch. For crisp seams, starch fabric before cutting and sewing. You can use special brands found at the fabric store or the kind you find at the supermarket— both work well.

Fine Pins. My favorite pins are Clover Flower Head Fine .45 mm.

Thread. I use Aurifil 50-weight thread. It's a thin and strong 100% cotton thread, perfect for paper piecing.

Pincushions. I have one pincushion for pins and another one for sewing machine needles.

Seam Ripper. A good quality seam ripper is a must-have too! Clover makes a nice one.

Fabric Glue Stick. Use this to glue small pieces of fabric to the paper pattern.

Size 80 Sewing Needle. I prefer to use a new one for every paper-pieced block because paper foundation patterns dull needles.

Lightweight Copy Paper or Special Foundation Paper. There are lots of specialty papers available. Experiment with different ones to find your favorite. Copy paper works well too.

Embroidery Floss. My favorites are Aurifil and Finca.

Hand-Sewing Needles. It's good to have various sizes and types of needles on hand. Use Sharps for hand sewing, embroidery needles for embellishments, and Betweens for hand quilting.

Fabric Marking Pen or Pencil. I like water-soluble markers. Be sure to test on a scrap of fabric to make sure the marks will wash out.

Basting Pins. These are great for basting quilts together. They are safety pins with a slight curve, which makes it easier to pin through layers of fabric and batting.

Thread Catcher. Paper piecing requires a lot of trimming of fabric and thread. Keep a fun bowl on your sewing table to hold all of those scraps.

Specialty Items. You'll notice that I use some specialty items like Japanese fabrics, crochet bias tape, decorative ribbons, and zippers and zipper-pull charms for my projects. Below are a few of my favorite places to shop for these products.

- **Etsy:** etsy.com
- **Super Buzzy:** superbuzzy.com
- **Sunny Day Supply:** sunnydaysupply.com

HOW TO PAPER PIECE

1 Photocopy or trace the pattern onto foundation paper. Set your sewing machine stitch length to 16 to 18 stitches per inch. This will make it easy to remove the paper pattern after you finish sewing.

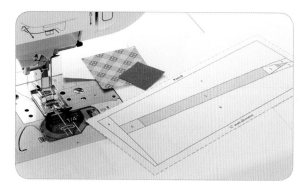

2 Flip the pattern over so the wrong (or unprinted) side is facing you. Place a piece of fabric, right side up, over section 1, making sure there is at least ½" of fabric around the perimeter of the section. Then turn the pattern to the right side as shown, and hold the foundation pattern up to a light source to help position the fabric. Pin or glue in place.

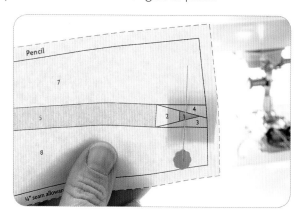

3 Flip the pattern over so the printed side of the pattern is facing you. Fold the pattern back on the line between sections 1 and 2. Trim the seam to ¼" using a rotary cutter and an acrylic ruler. This is your seam allowance.

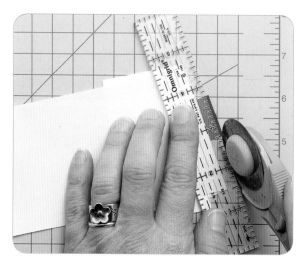

Folds Made Easy

I like to place the edge of a note card on the stitching line between sections and then fold the fabric over the edge of the card for a nice crisp fold.

4 Place fabric piece 2 right sides together with piece 1, aligning the raw edges. Pin in place along the seamline.

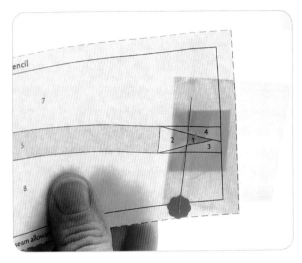

5 Fold the fabric over to make sure it covers section 2 entirely. Flip the fabric back over so the right sides of pieces 1 and 2 are facing each other.

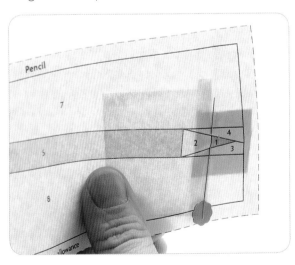

6 Flip the pattern over and stitch on the line between sections 1 and 2, backstitching at the beginning and end of the stitching.

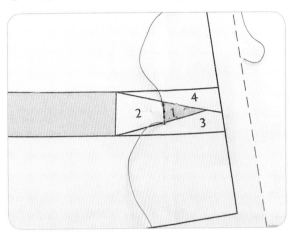

7 Open piece 2 so the right side of the fabric is showing. Press.

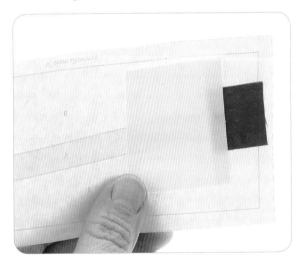

8 Add the remaining pieces of fabric in numerical order, using the method in steps 4–7. Trim the block ¼" beyond the pattern edge.

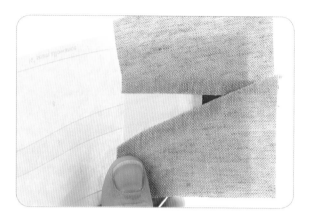

MATCHING SEAMS

Matching seams creates a professional-looking block and is not difficult with these simple tips!

1 Match the side seam of the waistband to the side seam of the apron.

2 Place the pieces right sides together. Pin through the seam intersections on the waistband and the corresponding seam on the apron body.

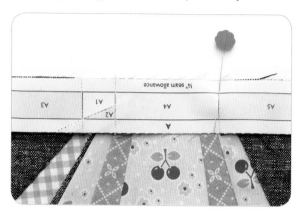

3 Change your stitch length to basting length (6 to 8 stitches per inch). Stitch, starting about ½" before the intersection of the seams and stopping about ½" beyond the intersection. Turn to the right side and check that the seams match. If they do, stitch over the basting stitch with a shorter stitch length. If they do not match, remove the basting stitch and baste again until your seams match.

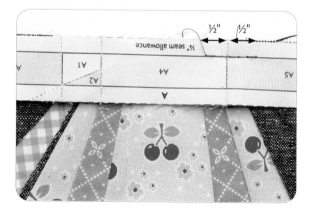

FUSSY CUTTING

1 Make an extra copy of the pattern. Cut the section of the pattern you want to fussy cut. For example, I want to fussy cut the waistband on the apron, section A4, with the word *queenbee*.

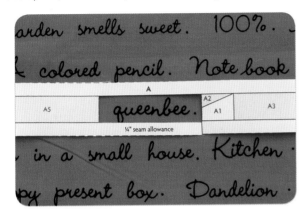

2 Place the pattern right side up on the wrong side of the fabric, covering the section you want to fussy cut. You may need to hold the fabric up to the light to help position the pattern. Use a bit of fabric glue to hold the pattern in place.

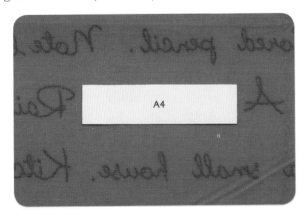

3 Using a see-through ruler, mark ¼" from the edge of your pattern. Cut on the line. Or use a rotary cutter and acrylic ruler to cut around the pattern, leaving a ¼" seam allowance.

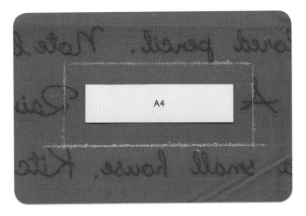

4 Remove the paper pattern from the back of the fabric. You now have a fussy-cut fabric piece to use in your block!

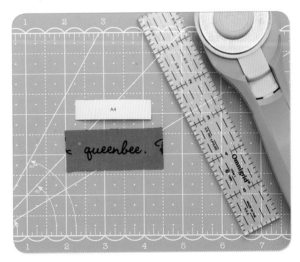

Colored-Pencil Pouch

The perfect beginning paper-pieced block, the colored pencil is made using one foundation pattern. Raid your scrap basket to make this pencil pouch with your favorite prints!

FINISHED BLOCK: 6½" × 2½"   **FINISHED POUCH:** 8½" × 4"

MATERIALS

Yardage is based on 42"-wide fabric.

1½" × 1½" square of red solid for pencil point

2" × 2" square of white solid for pencil wood

1" × 5½" rectangle of red print for pencil

1½" × 1½" square of pink print for eraser

¼ yard of natural linen for block background and pouch

⅛ yard of white dot for pouch

2 squares, 1½" × 1½", *each* of 6 different red prints for pouch

¼ yard (or fat eighth) of red print for lining and zipper tabs

¼ yard (or fat eighth) of fusible fleece

3½" length of ½"-wide ribbon or twill tape

9" nylon coil zipper

Zipper foot

Walking foot

CUTTING

All measurements include ¼" seam allowances.

From the natural linen, cut:
1 rectangle, 3" × 9"
2 rectangles, 1½" × 3"

From the white dot, cut:
5 squares, 2¾" × 2¾"; cut the squares into quarters
   diagonally to yield 20 side triangles
4 squares, 1¾" × 1¾"; cut the squares in half
   diagonally to yield 8 corner triangles

From the red print for lining and zipper tabs, cut:
2 rectangles, 4½" × 9"
2 rectangles, 1" × 3"

From the fusible fleece, cut:
2 rectangles, 4½" × 9"

PAPER PIECING THE BLOCK

Backstitch at the beginning and end of all seams.

1 Make one copy of the pencil foundation pattern
   on page 18.

2 Refer to "How to Paper Piece" on page 8 to
   foundation piece the Pencil block as follows:

- **Piece 1:** red solid
- **Piece 2:** white solid
- **Pieces 3, 4, and 7–9:** linen
- **Piece 5:** red print
- **Piece 6:** pink print

ASSEMBLING THE POUCH

Press the seam allowances as indicated by the arrows or as noted in the instructions.

1 Stitch one linen 1½" × 3" rectangle to each end of the pieced foundation. The block should measure 9" × 3", including the seam allowances. Remove the paper backing.

Make 1 block,
3" × 9".

2 Sew six red squares, 10 white large side triangles, and two white small corner triangles together into six units as shown.

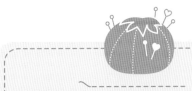

Working with Oversized Pieces

The triangles are oversized to allow for trimming to exact size after piecing. Align the right-angle corners as shown when stitching the triangles to the squares.

3 Join the units. Sew two white corner triangles to the pieced row. Press. Trim the pieced row to 2" × 9". Repeat to make a second pieced row.

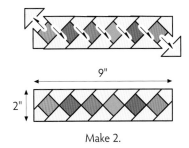

9"

2"

Make 2.

4 Sew one pieced row to the bottom of the pencil panel to complete the pouch front. Press. The pouch front should measure 4½" × 9", including the seam allowances.

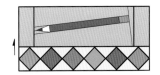

Make 1 pouch front,
4½" × 9".

5 Sew the remaining pieced strip to one long edge of the linen 3" × 9" rectangle to make the pouch back. Press the seam allowances toward the linen rectangle.

6 Fuse the fleece rectangles to the wrong side of the pouch front and back following the manufacturer's instructions.

7 Using a walking foot, stitch in the ditch around the pencil with matching red thread. Topstitch ¼" from the pieced strip on both the front and back linen rectangles.

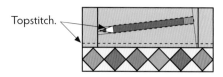

Topstitch.

ATTACHING THE ZIPPER

1 If your zipper is longer than 9", trim it as follows: make sure the zipper is closed. Measure 9" from the end of the zipper tape at the zipper-pull end, and mark. Take a few stitches by hand or (carefully) by machine across the zipper teeth, ¼" from the mark, to create a new zipper stop. Cut across at the mark.

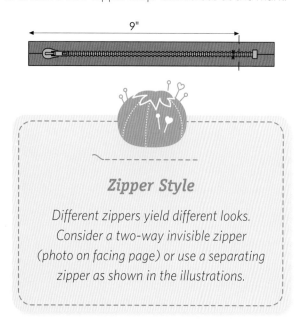

9"

Zipper Style

Different zippers yield different looks. Consider a two-way invisible zipper (photo on facing page) or use a separating zipper as shown in the illustrations.

2 Fold the ends of each red 1" × 3" rectangle ¼" toward the wrong side. Press. Press the rectangles in half, wrong sides together, to make zipper tabs.

¼"

3 Place one end of the zipper inside a folded zipper pull with the ends of the zipper tape at the center fold line. Pin in place. Stitch the zipper pull with an edge stitch, enclosing the zipper inside. Repeat for the other end of the zipper.

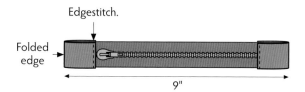

Edgestitch.

Folded edge

9"

4 Place the zipper on the pouch front, right sides together, aligning the top edges. Using a zipper foot, machine baste the zipper in place, starting and stopping ¼" from the side edges and backstitching at each end of the seam.

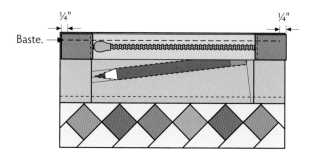

¼"   ¼"

Baste.

5 Fold the ribbon in half. Align the raw edges of the ribbon with the raw edge on the left side of the pouch front, placing the ribbon 1½" from the top raw edge. Baste the ribbon in place.

6 Place one 4½" × 9" red lining rectangle on the pouch front, right sides together, aligning the top edges. Using a zipper foot, stitch ¼" from the top edge, stopping ¼" from the side edges of the panel. Backstitch at the beginning and end of the stitching.

7 Repeat to sew the pouch back and remaining 4½" × 9" red lining rectangle to the opposite side of the zipper. Press the pouch and lining pieces away from the zipper. Topstitch ¼" from the zipper seam on the front and back pouch sections, starting and stopping ¼" from the side edges of the pouch.

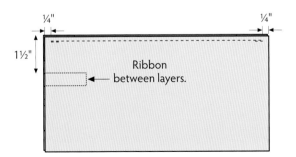

¼"   ¼"

1½"

Ribbon between layers.

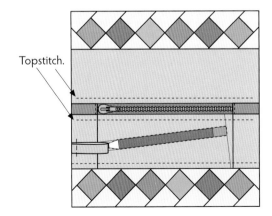

Topstitch.

FINISHING THE POUCH

1 Separate the lining pieces from the pouch pieces. Place the pouch pieces right sides together, matching seams and raw edges. Place the lining pieces right sides together, matching seams and raw edges. The zipper should face toward the lining. Fold the lining out of the way, toward the center of the lining pieces, and pin. Make sure the zipper is open so you can turn the purse right side out.

2 Sew the pouch pieces together, starting at the folded edge on the zipper end and backstitching at the ends. Unpin the lining pieces at each end of the zipper. Then pin and sew the lining pieces together, starting just below the zipper coils and leaving a 4" opening in the bottom for turning. Clip all corners. Turn the pouch right side out through the opening; press. Hand or machine sew the lining opening closed.

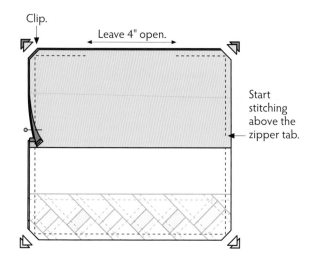

Clip.

Leave 4" open.

Start stitching above the zipper tab.

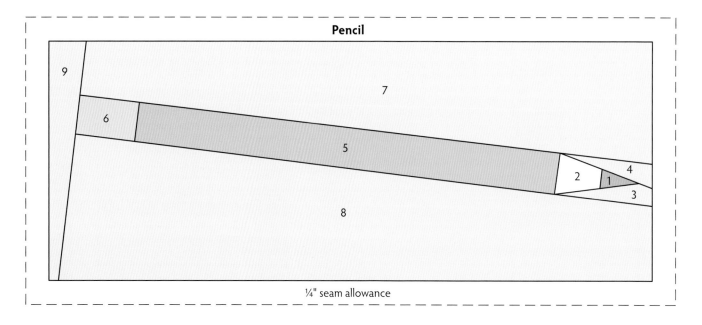

Pencil

9

7

6

5

2

4

1

3

8

¼" seam allowance

Sewing Cottage Pillow

Fussy cutting is one of my favorite techniques to use in paper-pieced blocks. Sewing-themed images fill this house, but the project can be customized to your interests. Let your imagination run wild. Make a cooking house or a gardening house or…. The possibilities are endless!

FINISHED BLOCK: 9" × 9"   FINISHED SIZE: 12" × 12"

MATERIALS

Yardage is based on 42"-wide fabric.

2½" × 6½" rectangle of brown scallop print for cottage roof

½ yard of white dot for background

6 fussy-cut motif squares, 2" × 2"*

10" × 10" square of yellow solid for curtains

1 fat eighth (9" × 21") of aqua gingham for house

1½" × 3" rectangle of yellow scallop print for porch roof

10" × 10" square of yellow dot for door and windowsills

7" × 7" square of green print for grass

3½" × 3½" square of aqua text print for sidewalk

¼ yard of pink floral for borders

*Make sure the images are small enough for windows.

Continued on page 21

Continued from page 19

1 fat quarter (18" × 21") of pink print for border
   corners and pillow back
1½ yards of ⅜"-wide double-fold bias tape *OR*
   1 fat quarter of fabric for binding**
12½" × 12½" square of muslin for pillow backing
12½" × 12½" square of cotton batting
Pillow form, 12" × 12" square

***To learn how to make bias binding, see my tutorial
at ChariseCreates.blogspot.com.*

CUTTING

All measurements include ¼" seam allowances.

From the white dot, cut:
1 strip, 1¾" × 9½"
2 rectangles, 2¼" × 6¾"
2 strips, ¾" × 5⅛"

From the aqua gingham, cut:
1 rectangle, ⅞" × 5½"

From the green print, cut:
1 I piece
1 J piece

From the aqua text print, cut:
1 K piece

From the pink floral, cut:
4 strips, 1¾" × 9½"

From the pink print, cut:
2 rectangles, 9" × 12"
4 squares, 1¾" × 1¾"

PAPER PIECING THE BLOCK

Backstitch at the beginning and end of all seams.

1 Make one copy *each* of the foundation patterns
for units A, B, C, D, E, F, G, and H on pattern
sheet 1.

2 Refer to "How to Paper Piece" on page 8
to foundation piece as follows:

UNIT A

- **Piece 1:** brown scallop print
- **Pieces 2–4:** white dot

UNIT C

- **Piece 1:** fussy-cut print
- **Pieces 2 and 3:** yellow solid
- **Pieces 4 and 5:** aqua gingham

UNITS B AND D

- **Piece 1:** fussy-cut print
- **Pieces 2 and 3:** yellow solid
- **Pieces 4:** aqua gingham

UNIT E

- **Piece 1:** yellow scallop
- **Pieces 2 and 3:** aqua gingham

Continued on page 22

Continued from page 21

UNIT G

- **Piece 1:** fussy-cut print
- **Pieces 2–4 and 7:** yellow dot
- **Pieces 5, 6, 8, and 9:** aqua gingham

UNITS F AND H

- **Piece 1:** fussy-cut print
- **Pieces 2–5:** yellow solid
- **Piece 6:** yellow dot
- **Pieces 7 and 8:** aqua gingham

ASSEMBLING THE BLOCK

Press the seam allowances as indicated by the arrows or as noted in the instructions.

1 Join units B, C, and D as shown.

Window section

2 Join units F, G, and H as shown.

    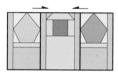

Door section

3 Join units B/C/D, E, and F/G/H as shown. Stitch the aqua gingham ⅞" × 5½" strip to the top.

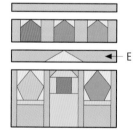 

4 Stitch the two white dot ¾" × 5⅛" strips to the sides. Press the seam allowance toward the strips. Stitch the A unit to the top to complete the block. Press the seam allowances toward the bottom.

The block should measure 6" × 6¾", including the seam allowances. Remove the paper backing.

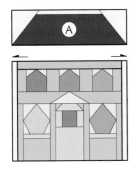

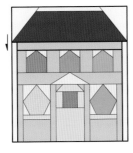

Make 1 cottage unit, 6" × 6¾".

ASSEMBLING THE PILLOW FRONT

1 Referring to the diagram below, stitch the white dot 2¼" × 6¾" rectangles to the sides of the cottage and the white dot 1¾" × 9½" strip to the top.

2 Join the green J piece, aqua text print K piece, and green L piece to make the path unit. Stitch it to the bottom of the cottage. The block should measure 9½" square, including the seam allowances.

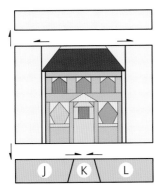

Block assembly

3 Stitch two pink floral 1¾" × 9½" strips to the top and bottom of the cottage block.

4 Stitch two pink print 1¾" squares to one pink floral 1¾" × 9½" strip to make a side border. Press the seam allowances toward the strip. Make two side borders. Add the side borders to the sides of the pillow front. The pillow front should measure 12" square, including the seam allowances.

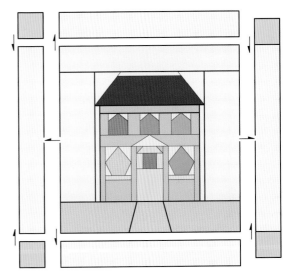

Pillow-top assembly

QUILTING THE PILLOW FRONT

1 Layer the muslin square, batting square, and pillow top. Baste the layers together.

2 Quilt in the ditch around the border, house, windows, doors, grass line, and path. Trim the muslin and batting even with the edge of the pillow front.

MAKING THE PILLOW BACK

1 Press ½" on the long side of one pink print
9" × 12" rectangle toward the wrong side. Fold
over ½" again, and press. Edgestitch to make a hem.
Repeat for the remaining backing rectangle.

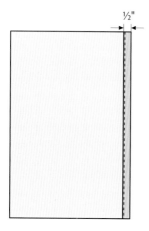

2 Place the pillow back pieces on the pillow front,
wrong sides together, overlapping the backing
rectangles to make the backing the same size as
the pillow front. Baste ¼" from the edges.

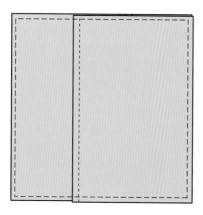

3 Place the corner template (pattern on
pattern sheet 1) on each corner. Mark the
corner and cut.

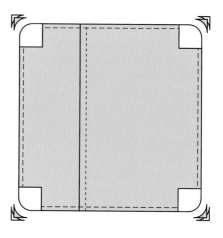

BINDING THE PILLOW

1 Press one end of the bias binding ⅜" toward the
wrong side. Place the folded end of the bias
binding on the right side of the pillow back at the
center bottom, aligning the raw edges. Pin in place.

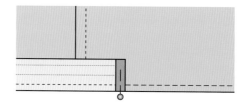

2 Stitch the binding to the pillow back. When you reach the starting point, overlap the folded end by ⅜" and trim the excess binding.

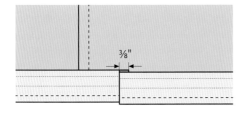

3 Fold the binding to the pillow front and fold under the raw edge ¼". The binding should just cover the stitching. Pin in place. Press. Hand slip-stitch or machine stitch the binding to the front of the pillow.

Choosing Prints

Small-scale prints create lovely blocks. Large-scale prints will get lost in the smaller elements of these blocks. Florals, geometrics, and conversational prints can add fun and whimsy to your blocks. Small-scale dots no larger than ⅛" and tiny ginghams are also good choices.

Apple Wristlet

This cute little wristlet purse, with its detachable handle, is the perfect size for your essentials. Ribbon and lace embellishments add a vintage touch.

FINISHED BLOCK: 4⅛" × 4¾"   FINISHED SIZE: 10½" × 7¾" (excluding strap)

MATERIALS

Yardage is based on 42"-wide fabric.

1½" × 2¼" rectangle of brown print for stem

⅓ yard of natural linen for block background and wristlet

¼ yard of green print for apple skin, zipper tabs, and lining

2" × 2½" rectangle of light green print for leaf

2¾" × 4" rectangle of white print for apple center

½ yard of 20"-wide lightweight fusible interfacing

¼ yard of 36"-wide fusible fleece

Brown embroidery floss

⅔ yard of ½"- to ⅝"-wide ribbon

⅔ yard of ½"-wide lace

9" nylon coil zipper

¾" D-ring

¾" swivel clasp

Water-soluble fabric pen or pencil

Zipper foot

CUTTING

All measurements include ¼" seam allowances.
The template for the bag piece is on pattern sheet 1.

From the natural linen, cut:

1 bag piece

2 rectangles, 4" × 5¼"

1 strip, 2⅜" × 11⅝"

1 strip, 2" × 12"

1 strip, 1⅞" × 11⅝"

1 rectangle, 2" × 2½"

From the green print, cut:

2 bag pieces

2 rectangles, 1" × 3¼"

From the interfacing, cut:

2 bag pieces

1 strip, 2" × 12"

1 rectangle, 2" × 2½"

From the fusible fleece, cut:

2 bag pieces

PAPER PIECING THE BLOCK

Backstitch at the beginning and end of all seams.

1 Make 1 copy *each* of the foundation patterns for units A, B, C, and D on pattern sheet 1.

2 Refer to "How to Paper Piece" on page 8 to foundation piece as follows:

UNIT A

- **Piece 1:** brown print
- **Pieces 2 and 3:** linen

UNIT B

- **Piece 1:** green print
- **Pieces 2–7:** linen

UNIT C

- **Piece 1:** light green print
- **Pieces 2–9:** linen

UNIT D

- **Piece 1:** white print
- **Pieces 2–8:** green print
- **Pieces 9–14:** linen

ASSEMBLING THE BLOCK

Press the seam allowances open unless otherwise indicated.

1 Join units A and B as shown. Join units C and D as shown.

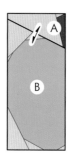 

2 Join units A/B and C/D as shown. The block should measure 4⅝" × 5¼", including the seam allowances. Remove the paper backing.

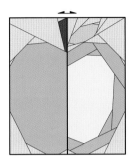

Make 1 block,
4⅝" × 5¼".

3 Mark the seed placement on the right side of the block using the pattern as a guide. Embroider the seeds with a lazy daisy stitch, using three strands of brown embroidery floss. For free, downloadable information on embroidery stitches, go to ShopMartingale.com/HowtoQuilt.

PREPARING THE PIECES

Referring to the manufacturer's instructions, fuse one interfacing bag piece to each green bag piece. Fuse the interfacing 2" × 2½" rectangle and 2" × 12" strip to the corresponding linen pieces.

ASSEMBLING THE FRONT AND BACK

1 Stitch the linen rectangles to the Apple block as follows and press all seam allowances toward the rectangles. Stitch the 4" × 5¼" rectangles to the sides of the Apple block. Stitch the 2⅜" × 11⅝" rectangle to the top and the 1⅞" × 11⅝" rectangle to the bottom. The pieced apple unit should measure 8½" × 11⅝", including the seam allowances.

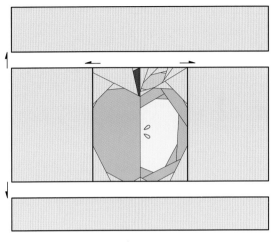

Make 1 unit,
8½" × 11⅝".

2 Place the bag template on the apple unit, centering the apple and aligning the top edges. Trace around the template. Cut on the line to make the wristlet front.

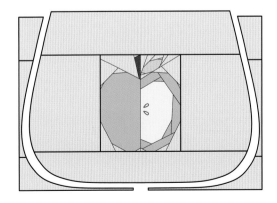

3 Iron one fusible fleece bag piece to the wrong side of the wristlet front, following the manufacturer's instructions. Repeat with the linen bag piece for the wristlet back.

4 Place the top edge of the ribbon 1" from the top edge of the wristlet front. Pin in place. Edgestitch along the top edge of the ribbon. Position the lace under the bottom edge of the ribbon, tucking ⅛" of the lace under the ribbon. Pin in place. Stitch the bottom edge of the ribbon, securing the lace with the stitching. Repeat for the wristlet back.

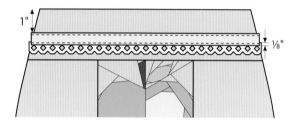

5 Stitch in the ditch around the apple, leaf, and stem with matching thread.

MAKING THE HANDLE TAB

1 Fold the linen 2" × 2½" handle tab in half lengthwise, wrong sides together. Press. Open the rectangle and fold under ¼" on each long edge. Press. Refold in half and edgestitch along both long edges.

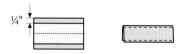

2 Slip the handle tab into the D-ring and fold the tab in half. Baste raw edges together as shown.

Baste.

MAKING THE HANDLE

1 Fold the linen 2" × 12" strip in half lengthwise, wrong sides together; press. Open the rectangle and fold under ¼" on each long edge; press.

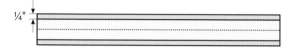

2 Thread the handle strip through the swivel clasp. With right sides together, join the ends of the strip. Finger-press the seam allowances open.

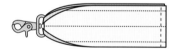

3 Refold the handle strip in half, keeping the ¼" edges on the inside. Pin in place. Edgestitch around each side of the handle. Position the handle so the seam is ¾" from the left end as shown. Using a zipper foot, stitch through all layers of the handle on the seam.

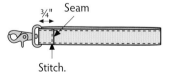

Seam

¾"

Stitch.

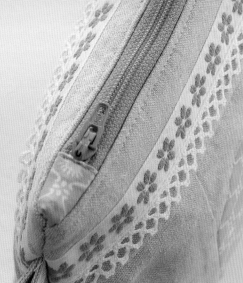

ADDING THE HANDLE AND DARTS

1 Place the handle tab on the left side of the wristlet front, 1" from the top raw edge. Baste in place.

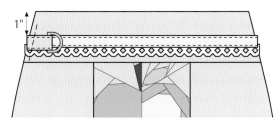

2 Stitch the darts in the wristlet front and back pieces, referring to "Stitching Darts" at right.

3 Stitch the darts in the green bag pieces and press in the same manner.

Stitching Darts

Start at the raw edge, backstitching at the beginning of the seam. Stitch, stopping ½" from the point, and change the stitch length to 15 stitches per inch. Finish the seam. Press the darts toward the center. Repeat for the other side, pressing the darts toward the side seam.

ATTACHING THE ZIPPER

1 Press the ends of each green 1" × 3¼" rectangle ¼" to the wrong side. Press the rectangle in half, wrong sides together, to make the zipper tabs.

2 Make sure the zipper is closed. Measure 9" from the end of the zipper tape at the zipper-pull end and mark. By hand or carefully by machine, take a few stitches across the zipper teeth, ¼" from the mark, to create a new zipper stop. Cut across at the mark.

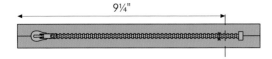

3 Place one end of the zipper inside a folded zipper pull with the end of the zipper tape at the center fold line. Pin in place. Stitch the zipper pull with an edge stitch, enclosing the zipper inside. Repeat for the other end.

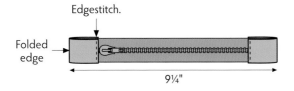

4 Place the zipper face down on the top edge of the right side of the wristlet front, right sides together. Place the long edge of the zipper tape even with the top edge of the front piece; pin in place. Using a zipper foot, stitch ¼" from the top edge, starting and stopping ⅜" from the edge, and backstitching at the ends.

5 Lay the wristlet front on one green bag piece, right sides together, matching the top raw edges; pin. The zipper will be between the front piece and the green lining. Stitch ¼" from the raw edge, following the stitching that attaches the zipper to the front piece. Start and stop stitching ⅜" from the side edges, backstitching at the ends of the seam.

6 Fold the lining over the zipper. The wristlet front and lining will be wrong sides together. Press both pieces away from the zipper. Topstitch ¼" away from the seam, stopping and starting ⅜" from the side edges; backstitch at the ends.

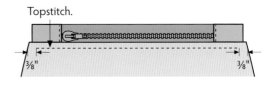

7 Repeat steps 4–6 for the back of the wristlet.

FINISHING THE WRISTLET PURSE

1 Separate the lining pieces from the wristlet pieces. Place the wristlet pieces right sides together, matching the side seams and darts. The zipper should face the lining. Pin in place. Fold the lining out of the way toward the center of the lining pieces and pin in place. Make sure the zipper is open so you can turn the wristlet right side out. Stitch ⅜" from the edge, starting at the top folded edge of the zipper tab and backstitching at the ends of the seam. Clip small triangles into the curved edges on the bottom corners of the wristlet. Press.

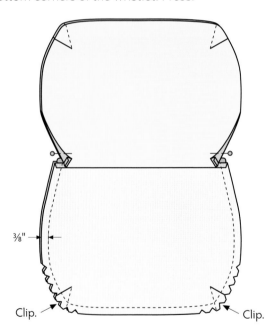

⅜"

Clip.   Clip.

2 Unpin the lining pieces at each end of the zipper. Place the lining right sides together, matching the side seams and darts. Start stitching with a ⅜" seam allowance, just below the top of the zipper tabs on the wristlet pieces, leaving a 5" opening in the bottom for turning and backstitching at the ends of the seam. Clip the bottom corner curves. Press.

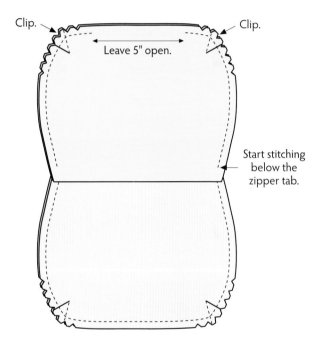

Clip.   Clip.

Leave 5" open.

Start stitching below the zipper tab.

3 Turn the wristlet right side out and press. Slip-stitch or machine edgestitch the opening in the lining.

Butterfly Cross-Body Bag

I love making practical items with paper-pieced blocks. The Butterfly Cross-Body Bag is a favorite of mine. It's the perfect size to carry essentials, and the cross-body strap makes it an easy-to-wear accessory.

FINISHED BLOCK: 6" × 4¾"   FINISHED SIZE: 7¼" × 7½" (excluding strap)

MATERIALS

Yardage is based on 42"-wide fabric.

⅝ yard of linen for purse
⅓ yard of fabric for lining
2 squares, 3½" × 3½", of yellow print A for wings
2 squares, 3½" × 3½", of yellow print B for wings
⅛ yard of aqua gingham for wings
1½" × 4" rectangle of gray print for body
Light gray embroidery floss
1 yard of yellow piping
1¼ yards of 20"-wide medium-weight interfacing
Water-soluble fabric pen or pencil
Heavy-duty sewing-machine needle
Zipper foot
Walking foot

CUTTING

All measurements include ¼" seam allowances.

From the linen, cut:

1 strip, 3¾" × 40¾"
1 strip, 1¾" × 23¼"
2 rectangles, 8" × 8¼"
1 rectangle, 7" × 7½"
1 strip, 1⅝" × 7½"
1 strip, 1⅛" × 7½"
2 strips, 1" × 5¼"

From the fabric for lining, cut:

2 rectangles, 8" × 8¼"
1 strip, 1¾" × 23¼"

From the interfacing, cut:

4 rectangles, 8" × 8¼"
2 rectangles, 7" × 7½"
1 strip, 3¾" × 40¾"
2 strips, 1¾" × 23¼"

APPLYING THE INTERFACING

1 Fuse an interfacing 8" × 8¼" rectangle to the wrong side of each linen 8" × 8¼" purse rectangle and each 8" × 8¼" lining rectangle.

2 Fuse an interfacing 7" × 7½" rectangle to the wrong side of the linen 7" × 7½" flap rectangle.

3 Fuse an interfacing 1¾" × 23¼" strip to the wrong side of the linen 1¾" × 23¼" strip and lining 1¾" × 23¼" strip.

4 Fuse the interfacing 3¾" × 40¾" strip to the wrong side of the linen 3¾" × 40¾" strip.

PAPER PIECING THE BLOCK

Backstitch at the beginning and end of all seams.

1 Make 1 copy *each* of the foundation patterns for units A, B, C, D, and E on pattern sheet 1.

2 Refer to "How to Paper Piece" on page 8 to foundation piece as follows:

UNITS A AND C

- **Piece 1:** yellow print A
- **Pieces 2–7:** aqua gingham
- **Pieces 8–12:** linen

UNITS B AND D

- **Piece 1:** yellow print B
- **Pieces 2–7:** aqua gingham
- **Pieces 8–13:** linen

UNIT E

- **Piece 1:** gray print
- **Pieces 2–5:** linen

ASSEMBLING THE BLOCK

Press the seam allowances open unless otherwise indicated by the arrows.

1 Join units A and B as shown. Join units C and D.

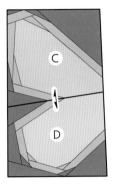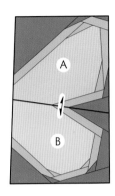

2 Join the wing sections to body unit E as shown. The block should measure 5¼" × 6½", including the seam allowances.

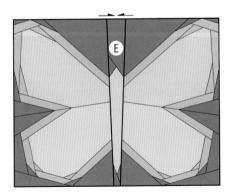

3 Stitch the linen 1" × 5¼" strips to the sides of the block. Stitch the linen 1⅝" × 7½" strip to the top and the linen 1⅛" × 7½" strip to the bottom. Press the seam allowances toward the strips. The flap unit should measure 7½" × 7", including the seam allowances. Remove the paper backing.

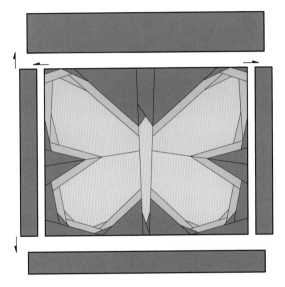

MAKING THE BAG FRONT AND BACK

1 Transfer the antenna lines (pattern sheet 1) to the Butterfly block. Using a backstitch, embroider the antennae with three strands of light gray embroidery floss.

3 1 2   Backstitch

2 Following the manufacturer's instructions, fuse the remaining interfacing 7" × 7½" rectangle to the wrong side of the finished flap unit.

3 Place the corner template (pattern sheet 1) on a bottom corner of the flap unit. Trace. Cut on the line. Repeat for the other bottom corner, as well as for the bottom corners of the linen 7" × 7½" rectangle.

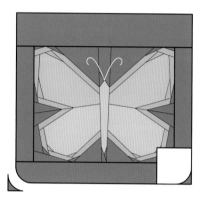

4 Place the piping on the right side of the flap unit, matching raw edges. Pin in place. Using a zipper foot, baste the piping to the sides and bottom close to the cording.

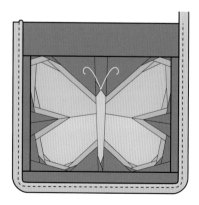

5 Place the trimmed flap unit on the trimmed linen 7" × 7½" rectangle, right sides together. Using a zipper foot, stitch the sides and bottom close to the cording, using the basting stitches as a guide. Clip the corners. Turn the flap right side out.

6 Fold the purse 8" × 8¼" front and back rectangles in half to find the center-bottom point. Mark. Fold the linen 1¾" × 23¼" gusset strip in half crosswise to find the center. Mark. Place the gusset on the purse front, right sides together, matching the center marks and top edges. Clip ¼" into the seam allowance on the bottom corners of the gusset. Pin the gusset to the purse front, matching raw edges. Stitch the seam using a ⅜" seam allowance. Repeat, stitching the other side of the gusset to the purse back.

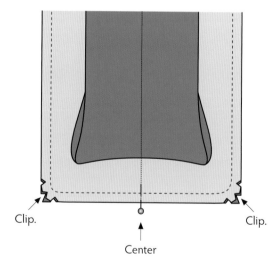

Clip.   Clip.

Center

7 Repeat step 6 for the lining, leaving a 4" opening in the purse bottom on one side of the gusset.

MAKING THE HANDLE

1 Fold the linen 3¾" × 40¾" strip in half lengthwise, wrong sides together; press. Open the strip and fold the long edges to the center; press. Refold and, using a heavy-duty needle and walking foot, edgestitch along both long edges.

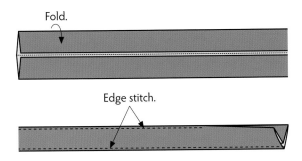

Fold.

Edge stitch.

2 Center the strap on the gusset of the purse, matching the raw edges as shown. Pin and baste in place. Repeat for the other side.

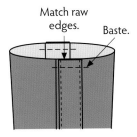

Match raw edges.

Baste.

3 Center the flap on the back of the purse, right sides together, aligning the top raw edges. Pin in place. Baste along top edge.

FINISHING THE PURSE

1 With the purse body right side out and the lining inside out, place the body inside the lining, right sides together. Make sure the handle strap and flap are tucked between the purse body and lining. Match the top raw edges and side seams. Pin in place. Stitch around the top with a ⅜" seam allowance. Turn right side out and press. Topstitch with a ¼" stitch around the top edge.

2 Machine edgestitch or hand slip-stitch the opening in the lining closed.

Summer Fruit Coasters

Stitch easy fruit coasters to add color to your summertime table. Gingham bias binding adds a quaint detail.

FINISHED BLOCKS: 5" × 5" (strawberry) & 5" × 5" (cherry)   FINISHED SIZE: 5½" × 5½"

MATERIALS FOR BOTH COASTERS

Yardage is based on 42"-wide fabric.

1 square, 4½" × 4½", *each* of 2 red prints for
    strawberries

4 rectangles, 1½" × 1½", of green print for
    strawberry leaves

1 square, 2" × 2", *each* of 3 red prints for cherries

2" × 2¼" rectangle of green print for cherry leaf

⅛ yard of white solid for background

4" × 6" rectangle of white print for bottom of blocks

1¼ yards of ⅜"-wide double-fold bias tape *OR*
    1 fat quarter of fabric for bias binding*

2 squares, 5½" × 5½", of fabric for backing

2 squares, 5½" × 5½", of fusible fleece

Green embroidery floss

*To learn how to make bias binding, see my tutorial at ChariseCreates.blogspot.com.

CUTTING

All measurements include ¼" seam allowances.

From the white solid, cut:

1 rectangle, 2⅜" × 5½", for strawberry

2 rectangles, 1¼" × 2⅝", for strawberry

2 rectangles, 1¼" × 4¾", for cherry

1 E piece (pattern sheet 1)

From the white print, cut:

1 rectangle, 1½" × 5½", for strawberry

1 rectangle, 1¼" × 5½", for cherry

PAPER PIECING THE STRAWBERRY BLOCKS

Backtrack at the beginning and end of all seams.

1 Make 1 copy *each* of the foundation patterns for units A, B, C, and D on pattern sheet 1.

2 Refer to "How to Paper Piece" on page 8 to foundation piece as follows:

UNIT A

- **Piece 1:** red print
- **Pieces 2–4, 6, and 8–10:** white solid
- **Pieces 5 and 7:** green print

UNIT B

- **Piece 1:** red print that matches unit A
- **Pieces 2–6:** white solid

UNIT C

- **Piece 1:** red print
- **Pieces 2–5, 7, and 9–11:** white solid
- **Pieces 6 and 8:** green print for strawberry leaves

UNIT D

- **Piece 1:** red print that matches unit C
- **Pieces 2–6:** white solid

ASSEMBLING THE STRAWBERRY COASTER

Press the seam allowances as indicated by the arrows or as noted in the instructions.

1 Join units A and B. Join units C and D.

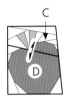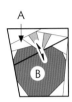

2 Join the strawberry units, the white solid E piece, and two white 1¼" × 2⅝" rectangles as shown. Press the seam allowances away from the foundations. Trim the unit to 5½" wide.

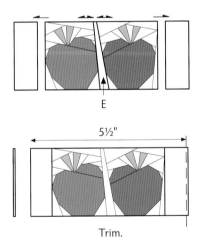

E

5½"

Trim.

3 Stitch the white print 1½" × 5½" rectangle to the bottom of the strawberry unit and the white 2⅜" × 5½" rectangle to the top. Press the seam allowances toward the rectangles. The block should measure 5½" square, including seam allowances. Remove the paper backing.

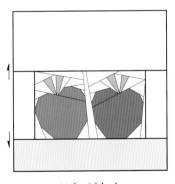

Make 1 block,
5½" × 5½".

ASSEMBLING THE CHERRY COASTER

1 Join units B, C, and D as shown. Press the seam allowances toward the left.

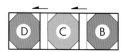

2 Join unit A and the cherry section. Press the seam allowances toward unit A. Stitch the white solid 1¼" × 4¾" rectangles to the sides of the unit. Press the seam allowances toward the rectangles. Stitch the white print 1¼" × 5½" rectangle to the bottom. Press the seam allowances toward the rectangle. Remove the paper backing.

PAPER PIECING THE CHERRY BLOCKS

1 Make one copy of the foundation pattern for units A, B, C, and D on pattern sheet 1.

2 Refer to "How to Paper Piece" on page 8 to foundation piece as follows:

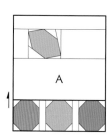
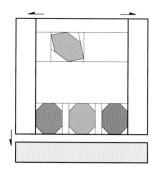

Make 1 block,
5½" × 5½".

UNIT A

- **Piece 1:** green print for cherry leaf
- **Pieces 2–11:** white solid

UNITS B AND C

- **Piece 1:** red print
- **Pieces 2–6:** white solid

UNIT D

- **Piece 1:** red print
- **Pieces 2–5:** white solid

3 Using the pattern as a guide, transfer the stems to the block. Stitch the stems with three strands of green embroidery floss and a short backstitch.

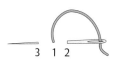
3 1 2

Backstitch

FINISHING THE COASTERS

1. Place the Strawberry block on a square of fusible fleece, with the fusible side of the fleece facing the back of the block. Fuse the block to the fleece following the manufacturer's instructions. Repeat for the Cherry block.

2. Stitch in the ditch around the fruit and leaves with matching thread.

3. Place each block on a backing square, wrong sides together. Baste ¼" from the raw edges.

4. Make a template of the corner pattern on pattern sheet 1. Trace the curved edge on each corner of the blocks, and trim on the lines.

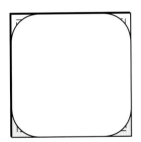 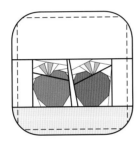

5. Fold one end of the binding strip ¼" toward the wrong side. Place the folded end of the binding on the coaster back at the center bottom, right sides together and raw edges aligned. Pin in place.

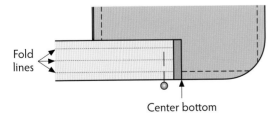

Fold lines

Center bottom

6. Stitch the binding to the back of the coaster using a ¼" seam allowance. When you reach the starting point, overlap the folded end by ⅜". Trim the excess binding.

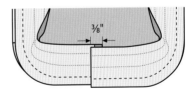

⅜"

7. Fold the binding to the right side of the coaster. Fold under ¼" along the raw edge so the binding just covers the stitching. Pin in place. Press. Hand slip-stitch or machine stitch the binding to the front of the coaster.

Summer Fruit Coasters

Vintage Apron Pouch

Create an adorable Vintage Apron block from just three pattern pieces. You'll take your skills to the next level and learn how to match seams perfectly. After you complete the block, make a fun zipper pouch that's perfect for carrying your hand-sewing projects.

FINISHED BLOCK: 6" × 6"   FINISHED SIZE: 10¼" × 9¼"

MATERIALS

Yardage is based on 42"-wide fabric.

4" × 4" square of blue gingham for apron bow

⅓ yard of gray linen for background

1½" × 3" rectangle of blue text print for waistband

10" × 10" square of pink print for apron

6" × 6" square of aqua print for apron

¼ yard of aqua text print for bottom border

⅓ yard of print for lining

⅓ yard of 36"-wide fusible fleece

⅔ yard of 20"-wide medium-weight fusible interfacing

14" nylon coil zipper

Zipper foot

Walking foot

Charm and split ring for zipper pull (optional)

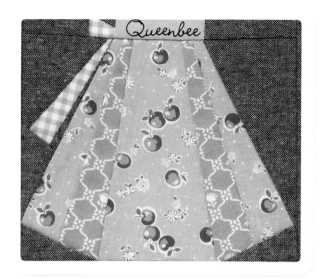

APPLYING THE INTERFACING

Fuse the interfacing rectangles to the wrong side of the 11" × 11¼" lining rectangles following the manufacturer's instructions.

PAPER PIECING THE BLOCK

Backstitch at the beginning and end of all seams.

1   Make 1 copy *each* of the foundation patterns for apron #1 units A, B, and C on pattern sheet 2.

2   Refer to "How to Paper Piece" on page 8 to foundation piece as follows:

UNIT A

- **Piece 1:** gingham
- **Pieces 2, 3, and 5:** linen
- **Piece 4:** blue text print (See "Fussy Cutting" on page 11.)

UNIT B

- **Piece 1:** gingham
- **Pieces 2–4:** linen

UNIT C

- **Pieces 1, 4, and 5:** pink print
- **Pieces 2 and 3:** aqua print
- **Pieces 6–8:** linen

CUTTING

All measurements include ¼" seam allowances.

From the print for lining, cut:
2 rectangles, 11" × 11¼"
2 rectangles, 1" × 3½"

From the gray linen, cut:
1 rectangle, 7¼" × 11"
1 strip, 1¼" × 11"
2 rectangles, 2¾" × 6½"
1 rectangle, 1¼" × 6½"

From the aqua text print, cut:
2 rectangles, 4½" × 11"

From the interfacing, cut:
2 rectangles, 11¼" × 11"

From the fusible fleece, cut:
2 rectangles, 11¼" × 11"

3 Join units A, B, and C as shown. Stitch the linen 1¼" × 6½" rectangle to the top. The block should measure 6½" square, including the seam allowances. Remove the paper backing. For perfectly matched seams, see "Matching Seams" on page 10.

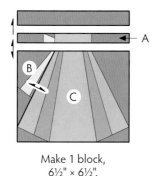

Make 1 block,
6½" × 6½".

ASSEMBLING THE POUCH FRONT AND BACK

Press the seam allowances as indicated by the arrows or as noted in the instructions.

1 Stitch the linen 2¾" × 6½" rectangles to the sides of the Vintage Apron block.

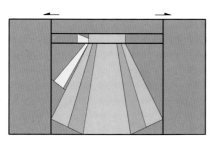

2 Stitch the linen 1¼" × 11" rectangle to the top of the block. Stitch one aqua text print 4½" × 11" rectangle to the bottom. Topstitch on the aqua print, ¼" from the bottom seam. The pouch front should measure 11" × 11¼", including the seam allowances.

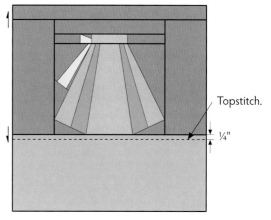

Topstitch.

¼"

Pouch front,
11" × 11¼".

3 To make the pouch back, stitch the linen 7¼" × 11" rectangle to the remaining aqua text print 4½" × 11" rectangle. Press the seam allowances toward the print rectangle. Topstitch on the aqua print ¼" from the seam. The pouch back should measure 11" × 11¼".

4 Fuse the fleece rectangles to the wrong side of the pouch front and back following the manufacturer's instructions.

5 Using a walking foot, quilt the block in the ditch around the apron.

ATTACHING THE ZIPPER

1 Press the ends of each lining 1" × 3½" rectangle ¼" to the wrong side. Press the rectangles in half, wrong sides together, to make zipper tabs.

¼"

2 Make sure the zipper is closed. Measure 11" from the end of the zipper tape at the zipper-pull end, and mark. Take a few stitches by hand or machine across the zipper teeth, ¼" from the mark, to create a new zipper stop. Cut across at the mark.

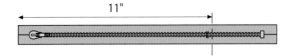

11"

3 Place one end of the zipper inside a folded zipper tab with the ends of the zipper tape at the center fold line. Pin in place. Stitch the tab close to the fold, enclosing the zipper inside. Repeat for the other end.

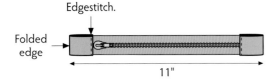

Edgestitch.

Folded edge

11"

4 Place the zipper face down on the right side of the pouch front. Align the edge of the zipper tape with the top edge of the pouch front, and pin in place. Using a zipper foot, stitch ¼" from the top edge, starting and stopping ⅜" from the side edges, and backstitching at the ends of the seam.

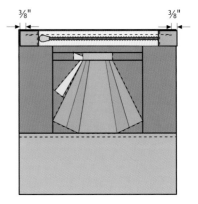

⅜"   ⅜"

5 Lay the pouch front on one 11" × 11¼" lining rectangle, right sides together, matching the top raw edges; pin. The zipper will be between the purse panel and lining. Stitch ¼" from the raw edge, following the stitching that attaches the zipper to the pouch panel. Start and stop stitching ⅜" from the side edges, backstitching at the ends of the seam.

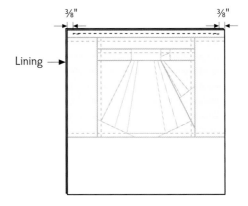

⅜"   ⅜"

Lining →

6 Fold the lining over the zipper. The pouch front and lining will be wrong sides together. Press both pieces away from the zipper. Topstitch ¼" away from the seam, stopping and starting ⅜" from the side edges, and backstitching at the ends of the seam.

Topstitch.

End stitching ⅜" from side edges.

7 Repeat steps 4–6 for the back of the pouch.

Zipping in Style

To add a bit of decoration to the zipper closure, I like to attach a charm to the zipper tab using a jump ring. If your local shop doesn't carry charms, have fun browsing online for just the right finishing touch.

FINISHING THE POUCH

1 Separate the lining pieces from the pouch pieces. Place the pouch pieces right sides together, matching the side seams and bottom edge. The zipper (which must be open!) should face the lining. Pin in place. Fold the lining out of the way and pin. Stitch ⅜" from the edge, starting at the top folded edge of the zipper tab, continuing around the perimeter, and backstitching at the ends.

2 Unpin the lining panels at each end of the zipper. Place the lining right sides together, matching the side seams. Stitch with a ⅜" seam allowance, just below the top of the zipper tabs on the pouch panels, leaving a 4" opening in the bottom for turning and backstitching at the ends.

3 To create the boxed bottom, fold the pouch corners right sides together, matching the side and bottom seams. Press the seam allowances open. Draw a line 1½" from the point, perpendicular to the seamline. Stitch on the line. Trim ¼" beyond the stitching. Repeat for the other bottom corner and the lining corners.

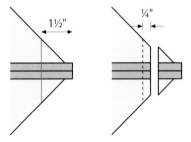

4 Turn the pouch right side out; press. Stitch the lining's opening closed by hand or machine.

5 Attach a charm to the end of the zipper pull if desired.

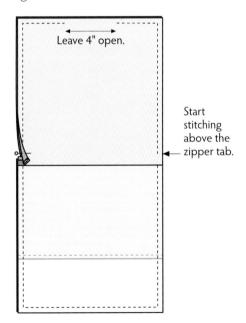

Leave 4" open.

Start stitching above the zipper tab.

Daisy Fabric Bowl

Stitch a pretty flower bowl to hold sewing notions or to use as an attractive jewelry holder on your dresser. The bowl is made from six paper-pieced petals that are hand stitched together.

FINISHED SIZE: 5¼" WIDE

MATERIALS

Yardage is based on 42"-wide fabric.

¼ yard of polka dot for background and inside bowl
¼ yard of yellow print for outside bowl and daisy center
⅛ yard of pink print A for daisy petals
⅛ yard of pink print B for daisy petals
¼ yard of 45"-wide fusible fleece
¼ yard of 20"-wide lightweight fusible interfacing
¼ yard of 20"-wide medium-weight fusible interfacing
1½" × 1½" square of cardstock or copy paper

CUTTING

All measurements include ¼" seam allowances. Patterns for A and C are on pattern sheet 2. Pattern for B is on pattern sheet 1.

From the polka dot, cut:

6 A petals

From the yellow print, cut:

6 A outside-bowl petals

1 B bowl bottom

1 C center

From the fusible fleece, cut:

1 B bowl bottom

6 A petals

From the lightweight interfacing, cut:

6 A petals

From the medium-weight interfacing, cut:

1 B bowl bottom

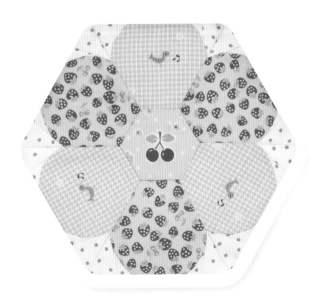

APPLYING THE INTERFACING

1   Fuse a fleece A piece to the wrong side of each polka-dot A piece following the manufacturer's instructions.

2   Fuse a lightweight interfacing A piece to the wrong side of each yellow print A piece following the manufacturer's instructions.

3   Fuse the medium-weight interfacing B piece to the wrong side of the yellow print B piece.

PAPER PIECING THE DAISY

Backstitch at the beginning and end of all seams.

1   Make six copies of the petal E foundation pattern on pattern sheet 2.

2   Paper piece six petals, making three from each pink print. Refer to "How to Paper Piece" on page 8 to foundation piece the petals as follows:

- **Piece 1:** pink print
- **Pieces 2–9:** polka dot

CONNECTING THE PETALS

Press the seam allowances open unless otherwise indicated in the instructions. Stitch the foundation-pieced petals together into two sections as shown. (See "Matching Seams" on page 10.) Pin the petal units together, matching the center points. Stitch the units together. Remove the paper backing.

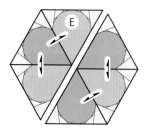 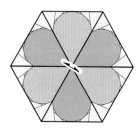

MAKING THE HEXAGON CENTER

1 Cut the D hexagon out of cardstock or copy paper.

2 Center the cardstock template on the wrong side of the yellow print C piece. Use fabric glue to secure the template in place.

3 Thread a needle and knot the end. Fold two adjacent fabric seam allowances over the hexagon template. Baste the seam allowances together where they overlap as shown. Secure the thread with a backstitch.

4 Move to the next corner and baste the seam allowances together. Baste the seam allowances together around the template in the same manner.

5 Press the hexagon on the wrong side using a dry iron. Remove the thread and paper template. Press again on the right side.

6 Center the yellow hexagon on the daisy. Topstitch the hexagon to the flower close to the edges.

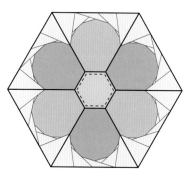

MAKING THE BOWL BOTTOM

1   Center the fusible-fleece B piece on the wrong side of the yellow bowl-bottom B piece. Fuse in place following the manufacturer's instructions.

2   Layer the daisy unit and the yellow B piece right sides together. Stitch the pieces together, following the edge of the fusible fleece and backstitching at the ends. Leave an opening on one side for turning. Trim the corners close to the stitching, except for the corners at either end of the opening.

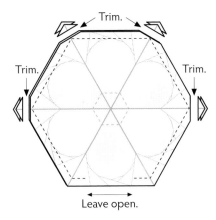

3   Press ¼" seam allowance toward the wrong side on each opening edge. Turn the bowl bottom right side out; press. Slip-stitch the opening closed.

MAKING AND ATTACHING THE PETALS

1   Place a polka-dot A petal and a yellow A petal right sides together. Stitch the petals together using a ¼" seam allowance, leaving the bottom open

and backstitching at the ends. Clip the curved edge. Turn the petal right side out. Fold the bottom edges ¼" toward the inside. Slip-stitch the bottom opening closed. Make six petals.

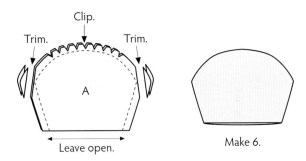

2   Hand stitch the petals to the bowl bottom with a tiny slip stitch.

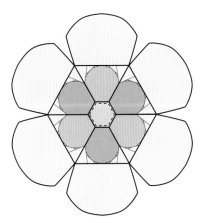

3   Join the petals along their side edges using a tiny slip stitch.

Rain, Rain, Go Away Purse

Rainy days don't have to be dreary when you carry this easy-to-make purse. It includes gingham and lace trim and has a long strap that can be thrown over one shoulder or angled for a cross-body bag. Two other great features are a magnetic clasp and an inside pocket.

FINISHED BLOCK: 8½" × 9"   **FINISHED SIZE:** 15" × 15½" (excluding strap)

MATERIALS

Yardage is based on 42"-wide fabric.

⅓ yard of aqua gingham for border and pocket

1¼ yard of linen for bag

5" × 5" square of charcoal print for umbrella handle and tip

⅛ yard of yellow stripe for umbrella

⅛ yard of yellow floral for umbrella

3 rectangles, 2" × 2¾", of aqua print for raindrops

2 rectangles, 2" × 2¾", of aqua check for raindrops

½ yard of print for lining

2 yards of 20"-wide medium-weight fusible interfacing

½ yard of 36"-wide fusible fleece

1 yard of ¾"- or ⅞"-wide lace

Continued on page 60

Continued from page 59

Magnetic clasp
Water-soluble fabric pen or pencil
Heavy-duty sewing-machine needle
Walking foot

CUTTING

All measurements include ¼" seam allowances.

From the aqua gingham, cut:
1 rectangle, 10¼" × 12½"
4 strips, 3¼" × 15½"

From the linen, cut:
1 rectangle, 12" × 15½"
1 strip, 6" × 41"
1 strip, 4¼" × 11¼"
1 strip, 3¼" × 11¼"
1 strip, 1¼" × 15½"
1 strip, 2¼" × 9"

From the print for lining, cut:
2 rectangles, 12" × 15½"

From the fusible fleece, cut:
2 rectangles, 12" × 15½"

From the interfacing, cut:
1 strip, 6" × 41"
2 rectangles, 12" × 15½"
4 strips, 3¼" × 15½"
2 squares, 1½" × 1½"

APPLYING THE INTERFACING

1 Fuse an interfacing 3¼" × 15½" strip to the wrong side of each aqua gingham strip.

2 Fuse the interfacing 6" × 41" strip to the wrong side of the linen 6" × 41" strip.

3 Fuse an interfacing 12" × 15½" rectangle to the wrong side of each lining 12" × 15½" rectangle.

PAPER PIECING THE BLOCKS

Backstitch at the beginning and end of all seams.

1 Make 1 copy *each* of the foundation patterns for section 1 units A, B, C, D, E, F and G; section 2 units A, B, and C; and section 3 unit A. The patterns are on pattern sheet 2.

2 Refer to "How to Paper Piece" on page 8 to foundation piece as follows:

Section 1

UNIT A

- **Piece 1:** charcoal print
- **Pieces 2 and 3:** linen

UNIT B

- **Pieces 1 and 5–7:** linen
- **Pieces 2–4:** yellow stripe

UNIT C

- **Piece 1:** linen
- **Pieces 2–4:** yellow floral

UNIT D

- **Piece 1:** linen
- **Pieces 2–4:** yellow stripe

UNIT E

- **Pieces 1 and 5–7:** linen
- **Pieces 2–4:** yellow floral

UNIT F

- **Pieces 1, 5, and 8–11:** linen
- **Pieces 2–4, 6, and 7:** charcoal print

UNIT G

- **Piece 1:** aqua print
- **Pieces 2–13:** linen

Section 2

UNIT A

- **Piece 1:** aqua check
- **Pieces 2–15:** linen

UNIT B

- **Piece 1:** aqua print
- **Pieces 2–13:** linen

UNIT C

- **Piece 1:** aqua check
- **Pieces 2–14:** linen

Section 3

UNIT A

- **Piece 1:** aqua print
- **Pieces 2–13:** linen

ASSEMBLING SECTION 1

Press the seam allowances as indicated by the arrows or as noted in the instructions.

1 Join units B, C, D, and E to make the umbrella section, pressing the seam allowances open after stitching each seam.

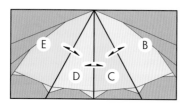

2 Stitch unit A to the top of the umbrella section and unit F to the bottom as shown. Stitch unit G to the left side. Press the seam allowance toward unit G. The block should measure 8" × 6½", including the seam allowances. Remove the paper backing.

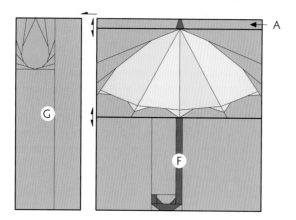

ASSEMBLING SECTION 2

Join units A, B, and C. The block should measure 8" × 3½", including the seam allowances. Remove the paper backing.

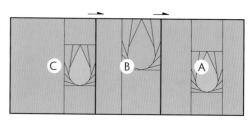

ASSEMBLING THE BLOCK

Join sections 1 and 2 as shown. Stitch section 3 to the right side. Press the seam allowances open. The block should measure 9" × 9½", including the seam allowances. Remove the paper backing.

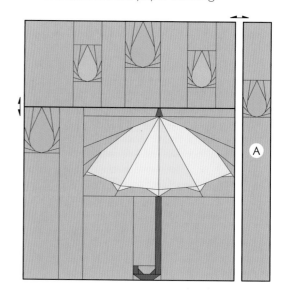

ASSEMBLING THE FRONT AND BACK

1 Stitch the linen 2¼" × 9" rectangle to the bottom of the block. Stitch the linen 4¼" × 11¼" rectangle to the left side of the block and the linen 3¼" × 11¼" rectangle to the right side. Stitch the linen 1¼" × 15½" strip to the top of the block.

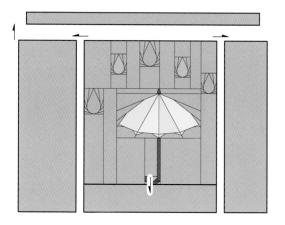

2 Fuse a fusible fleece rectangle to the wrong side of the pieced purse front following the manufacturer's instructions. Repeat for the linen 12" × 15½" rectangle for the purse back.

3 Quilt the umbrella and raindrops in the ditch with matching thread.

4 Place the lace on the purse front, aligning the top edges. Baste in place. Repeat for the back.

5 Place an aqua gingham 3¼" × 15½" strip on the purse front, right sides together, aligning the top edges. Pin in place; stitch. Edgestitch the seam on the border side. Repeat for the purse back.

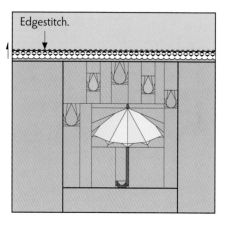

6 Place the corner template (see pattern sheet 2) on the purse front, aligning the bottom and side edges. Trace around the template. Cut on the line. Flip the pattern over and repeat for the other side of the front panel. Repeat for the purse back.

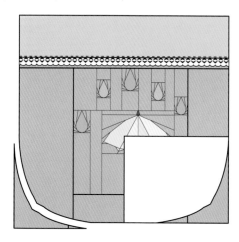

7 Stitch the darts, referring to "Stitching the Darts" below.

8 Place the purse front and back right sides together, aligning the raw edges, seams, and darts. Stitch around the purse with a ⅜" seam allowance, leaving the top open. Clip the corners. Turn right side out.

Stitching the Darts

Start at the raw edge, backstitching at the beginning of the seam. Stitch, stopping ½" from the point and changing the stitch length to 15 stitches per inch. Finish the seam. Press the darts toward the center. Repeat for the other side, pressing the darts toward the side seam.

ASSEMBLING THE LINING AND POCKET

1 Place an aqua gingham 3¼" × 15½" border strip on a lining 12" × 15½" rectangle aligning the top edges. Pin in place; stitch. Press the seam allowances toward the gingham. Edgestitch the seam on the gingham side. Repeat for the other lining rectangle.

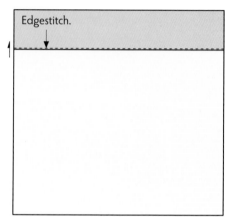

Edgestitch.

2 Fold the aqua gingham 10¼" × 12½" rectangle in half crosswise, right sides together. The folded edge will become the top edge of the pocket. Stitch the unfolded sides ¼" from the edges, leaving a 2" opening in the bottom. Turn right side out. Press.

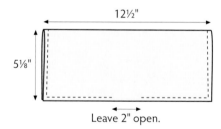

12½"

5⅛"

Leave 2" open.

3 Center the pocket on the purse lining, 1" from the border seam. Edgestitch the pocket sides and bottom, backstitching at the ends. Stitch a vertical line, 4" from the right edge, backstitching at the top edge.

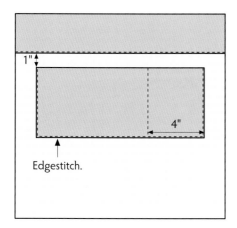

1"

4"

Edgestitch.

4 Fold one lining piece in half vertically to find the center. Measure 1⅜" from the top and mark the center on the wrong side. Fuse one interfacing 1½" square on the lining, centered over the mark. Attach the back of the magnetic clasp on the lining's right side at the center mark, following the manufacturer's instructions. Repeat for the other lining piece.

5 Finish the lining as described in "Assembling the Front and Back" on pages 63 and 64, steps 6–8, leaving a 4" opening along the bottom of the lining.

MAKING THE HANDLE

1 Fold the linen 6" × 41" strip in half lengthwise, wrong sides together; press. Open the strap;

press long edges to center. Refold; using a heavy-duty needle and walking foot, edgestitch both long edges.

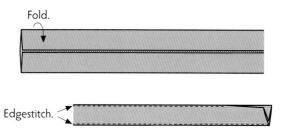

Fold.

Edgestitch.

2 Center the strap on the side seam of the purse, aligning raw edges; baste. Repeat for other side.

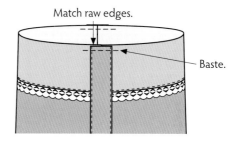

Match raw edges.

Baste.

FINISHING THE PURSE

1 With purse body right side out and lining inside out, place the body inside the lining, right sides together. Tuck the handle strap between the purse body and lining. Match the top raw edges and side seams. Pin; stitch around the top with a ⅜" seam allowance. Turn right side out; press. Topstitch ¼" from the top edge.

2 Stitch in the ditch of the border seam through all layers and then machine edgestitch the lining opening closed.

Garden Tote

Create a garden tote that combines whimsical fabrics with a fun paper-pieced block that becomes an outside pocket. I promise, this will be the first tote you grab when you're heading out on a shopping trip!

FINISHED BLOCK: 9½" × 5¼"   **FINISHED SIZE:** 20" wide × 15½" tall (excluding strap)

BLOCK MATERIALS

Yardage is based on 42"-wide fabric unless otherwise noted.

1 fat eighth of natural solid for block background

1 fat eighth *each* of yellow solid and yellow print for watering can

2¾" × 4" rectangle of red print for watering can

2¾" × 10" strip of red text print for pocket

⅝ yard of red gingham for tote bottom and binding*

¾ yard of 54"-wide natural cotton canvas for tote

3 yards of 1"-wide red cotton webbing

9½" × 10½" piece of cotton batting

Walking foot

Heavy-duty sewing-machine needle

*To learn how to make bias binding, see my tutorial at CharlseCreates.blogspot.com.

CUTTING

All measurements include ¼" seam allowances.

From the natural solid, cut:

1 strip, 1¾" × 10", for top of pocket

From the red gingham, cut:

1 rectangle, 12¾" × 20¾", for tote bottom exterior

1 rectangle, 9½" × 10½", for pocket lining

1 strip, 1½" × 42", on the bias for binding

2 strips, 1½" × 20", on the bias for binding

3 strips, 1½" × 10½", on the bias for binding

From the natural cotton canvas, cut:

2 rectangles, 13¾" × 20¾", for tote front and back

1 rectangle, 12¾" × 20¾", for tote bottom interior

From the cotton webbing, cut:

2 pieces, 52¾" long

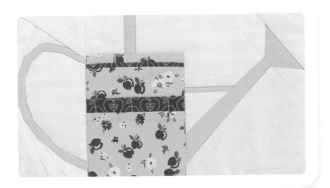

PAPER PIECING THE BLOCK

Backstitch at the beginning and end of all seams.

1. Make 1 copy *each* of the foundation patterns for units A, B, C, and D on pattern sheet 1.

2. Refer to "How to Paper Piece" on page 8 to foundation piece as follows:

UNIT A

- **Pieces 1 and 10–19:** natural solid

- **Pieces 2–9:** yellow solid

UNIT B

- **Piece 1:** yellow solid

- **Pieces 2 and 3:** natural solid

- **Pieces 4, 6, and 8:** yellow print

- **Pieces 5 and 7:** red print

UNIT C

- **Pieces 1 and 4:** yellow solid

- **Pieces 2, 3, and 5:** natural solid

UNIT D

- **Piece 1:** yellow solid

- **Pieces 2–4:** natural solid

ASSEMBLING THE BLOCK

Press the seam allowances as indicated by the arrows or as noted in the instructions.

1 Join units A and B as shown. Join units C and D as shown.

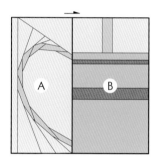 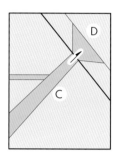

2 Join units A/B and C/D to complete the Watering Can block. The block should measure 10" × 5¾", including the seam allowances.

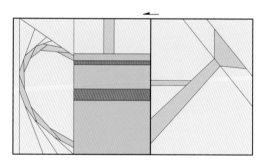

Make 1 block,
10" × 5¾".

MAKING THE POCKET

1 Stitch the red text 2¾" × 10" strip to the bottom of the block. Stitch the natural solid 1¾" × 10" strip to the top of the block. The pocket front should measure 10" × 9¼", including the seam allowances. Remove the paper backing.

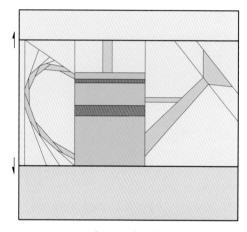

Make 1 pocket front,
10" × 9¼".

2 Layer the pocket front with the batting rectangle and red gingham 9½" × 10½" rectangle. Baste the layers together. Quilt in the ditch around the watering can and along the seam below the watering can with matching thread. Baste around the perimeter

¼" away from the raw edge. Trim the batting and red gingham even with the edges of the pocket front.

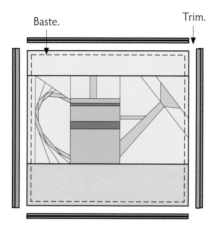

Baste.　　　　　　　　Trim.

3 Place one long edge of a 10½" length of bias binding ⅜" toward the wrong side. Place the binding on the wrong side of the pocket, right side down, aligning the unpressed edge with the top edge of the pocket. Stitch the binding to the pocket using a ⅜" seam allowance.

4 Fold the binding to the right side. Edgestitch in place. Trim the binding even with the edges of the pocket.

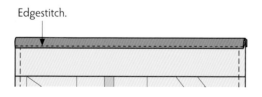

Edgestitch.

ASSEMBLING THE TOTE

1 Fold a canvas 13¾" × 20¾" rectangle in half crosswise. Mark center on bottom. Fold pocket in half; mark center. Place pocket on rectangle; match centers and raw edges. Pin. Baste ¼" from bottom.

2 Place a webbing strap on the canvas rectangle, covering ⅜" of pocket on both sides. Pin. There should be 9¼" between webbing edges. With a walking foot and heavy-duty needle in your machine, stitch webbing to the tote front. Start at the bottom and edgestitch webbing to the pocket and rectangle, stopping 1" above the pocket's top edge. Pivot, stitch across the webbing, pivot; edgestitch the other side of the webbing, encasing the raw edge of the pocket.

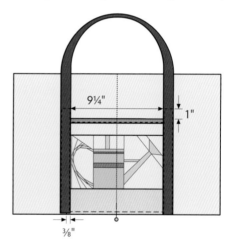

9¼"　　　1"

⅜"

3 Attach the remaining webbing strap to the other canvas 13¾" x 20¾" rectangle in the same way. Place the webbing 4⅝" from the center of the rectangle. There should be 9¼" between webbing edges. Edgestitch the webbing to the rectangle, stopping 10¼" above the bottom edge. Pivot, stitch across the webbing, pivot; edgestitch the other side..

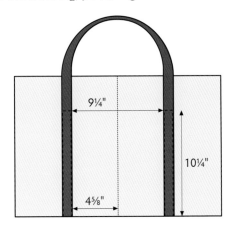

4 Place the tote back and the gingham 12¾" × 20¾" rectangle right sides together, aligning the bottom edges. Stitch ⅜" from the edge, backstitching at the ends. Repeat, sewing the opposite edge of the gingham to the bottom edge of the tote front.

5 Press the front and back tote-bag seam allowances toward the gingham. Flip over the panels so that the wrong side of the tote bag and canvas bottom are facing you.

6 Fold under ⅜" on the two long raw edges of the canvas bottom. Align one long folded edge with the seam joining the back panel and gingham bottom panel. Edgestitch the seam, backstitching at the ends. Repeat to edgestitch the remaining long edge.

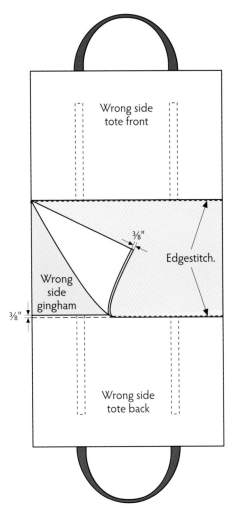

7 Place the tote front and tote back right sides together, matching the top and sides. Stitch the side seams with a ⅜" seam allowance.

8 Press one long edge of a gingham 20"-long bias strip ⅜" toward the wrong side. Place the strip on one side seam, aligning raw edges. Stitch with a ⅜" seam allowance. Fold the binding over the seam and topstitch the pressed edge to enclose the seam.

9 Create the boxed bottom; fold bag corners, right sides together, matching the side and bottom seams. Draw a line 3 from the point, perpendicular to seamline. Stitch on line. Trim ¼" beyond stitching. Repeat for other bottom corner. Bind the trimmed edges with the remaining gingham 10½"-long bias strips, folding ends ⅜" toward the wrong side.

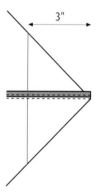

BINDING THE TOP EDGE

1 Fold one end of a 42"-long bias binding strip ⅜" toward the wrong side. Place the folded end of the bias binding at the side seam, with the right side of the binding on the inside of the tote, matching the raw edges. Pin in place.

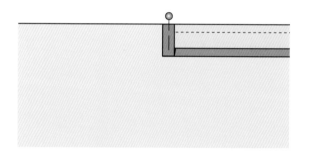

2 Stitch the binding to the bag. When you reach the starting point, overlap the binding over the folded edge by ⅜". Trim the excess binding.

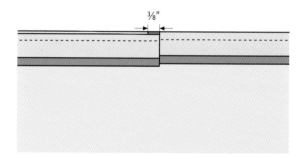

3 Fold the binding to the outside of tote, covering the stitching. Pin in place. Press. Hand slip-stitch or machine edgestitch the binding to the outside of the tote.

Clothesline Mini-Quilt

*Make a sweet mini-quilt, using your favorite fabrics, to
hang in your sewing room or to decorate a little girl's room.
A pinwheel border and colorful embroidery give it whimsy.*

FINISHED BLOCKS: 6" × 5¼" (aprons) & 5½" × 9" (dress)   FINISHED SIZE: 20½" × 20½"

MATERIALS

Yardage is based on 42"-wide fabric.

¼ yard of aqua floral for aprons and pinwheels

½ yard of white dot for background

2 rectangles, 3" × 1½", of aqua text print for apron
   waistband

¼ yard of aqua gingham for aprons and pinwheels

10" × 10" square of red gingham for dress bodice

4" × 4" square of red solid for dress sash

7" × 7" square of pink print for dress skirt

1 square, 3" × 3", *each of 2 red prints for pinwheels*

⅛ yard of white floral for pinwheels

1 square, 3" × 3", *each of 2 light pink prints for*
   pinwheels

Continued on page 75

Continued from page 73

2½ yards of ⅜"-wide double-fold bias tape *OR*
  1 fat quarter of aqua print for binding*
22" × 22" square of fabric for backing
22" × 22" square of cotton batting
Aqua, dark pink, and dark gray embroidery floss
Water-soluble fabric pen or pencil
Walking foot

*To learn how to make bias binding, see my tutorial
at ChariseCreates.blogspot.com.*

CUTTING

All measurements include ¼" seam allowances.

From the aqua floral, cut:

2 squares, 2⅝" × 2⅝"; cut the squares in half
  diagonally to yield 4 triangles

From the white dot, cut:

1 rectangle, 3¾" × 20½"
1 rectangle, 3¼" × 20½"
2 rectangles, 4¼" × 7¾"
2 rectangles, 1¾" × 5¾"
2 squares, 6½" × 6½"; cut the squares into quarters
  diagonally to yield 8 side triangles (2 are extra)
2 squares, 3¾" × 3¾"; cut the squares in half
  diagonally to yield 4 corner triangles

From the aqua gingham, cut:

2 squares, 2⅝" × 2⅝"; cut the squares in half
  diagonally to yield 4 triangles

From *each* red print 3" square, cut:

1 square, 2⅝" × 2⅝"; cut the squares in half
  diagonally to yield 2 triangles (4 total)

From the white floral, cut:

8 squares, 2⅝" × 2⅝"; cut the squares in half
  diagonally to yield 16 triangles

From *each* light pink print 3" square, cut:

1 square, 2⅝" × 2⅝"; cut the squares in half
  diagonally to yield 2 triangles (4 total)

PAPER PIECING THE APRON #1 BLOCK

Backstitch at the beginning and end of all seams.

1 Make 1 copy *each* of the foundation patterns for
  apron #1 units A, B, and C on pattern sheet 2.

2 Refer to "How to Paper Piece" on page 8 to
  foundation piece as follows:

UNIT A

- **Piece 1:** aqua floral
- **Pieces 2, 3, and 5:** white dot
- **Piece 4:** aqua text print (See "Fussy Cutting" on page 11)

UNIT B

- **Piece 1:** aqua floral
- **Pieces 2 –4:** white dot

UNIT C

- **Pieces 1, 4, and 5:** aqua gingham
- **Pieces 2 and 3:** aqua floral
- **Pieces 6-8:** white dot

PAPER PIECING THE APRON #2 BLOCK

1 Make 1 copy *each* of the foundation patterns for apron #2 units A, B, and C on pattern sheet 2.

2 Refer to "How to Paper Piece" on page 8 to foundation piece as follows:

UNIT A

- **Piece 1:** aqua gingham
- **Pieces 2, 3, and 5:** white dot
- **Piece 4:** aqua text print (See "Fussy Cutting" on page 11)

UNIT B

- **Piece 1:** aqua gingham
- **Pieces 2-4:** white dot

UNIT C

- **Pieces 1, 4, and 5:** aqua floral
- **Pieces 2 and 3:** aqua gingham
- **Pieces 6-8:** white dot

PAPER PIECING THE DRESS BLOCK

1 Make 1 copy *each* of the foundation patterns for the dress units A, B, C, and D on pattern sheet 2.

2 Refer to "How to Paper Piece" on page 8 to foundation piece as follows:

UNIT A

- **Pieces 1 and 4-7:** white dot
- **Pieces 2 and 3:** red gingham

UNIT B

- **Pieces 1 and 4-6:** white dot
- **Pieces 2 and 3:** red gingham

UNIT C

- **Piece 1:** red solid
- **Pieces 2-4:** white dot

UNIT D

- **Piece 1:** red solid
- **Pieces 2-4 and 6-8:** white dot
- **Piece 5:** pink print

ASSEMBLING THE BLOCKS

Press the seam allowances as indicated by the arrows or as noted in the instructions.

1. For apron #1, join units B and C as shown. Press the seam allowances toward unit C. Stitch unit A to unit B/C. The block should measure 6½" × 5¾", including the seam allowances. Repeat for apron #2. Remove the paper backing.

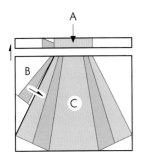 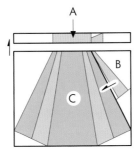

Apron #1.
Make 1 block,
6½" × 5¾".

Apron #2.
Make 1 block,
6½" × 5¾".

2. Join dress foundations B and C as shown. Press the seam allowances toward unit B.

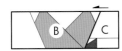

3. Join units A, B/C, and D to complete the Dress block. Press the seam allowances away from unit B/C. The completed block should measure 6" × 9½", including the seam allowances. Remove the paper backing.

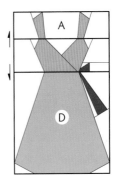

Make 1 dress block, 6" × 9½".

ASSEMBLING THE PINWHEEL BORDER

Press the seam allowances open unless otherwise indicated by the arrows.

1. Stitch a red print triangle to a white floral triangle to make a half-square triangle unit as shown. Trim the unit to 2¼" square.

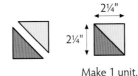

Make 1 unit.

2 Repeat to make a total of four red, four light pink, and eight aqua half-square triangle units.

3 Lay out two different light pink half-square-triangle units and two different red print half-square triangle units as shown. Join the units into two rows. Join the rows. The Pinwheel block should measure 4" square, including the seam allowances. Make two pink and red Pinwheel blocks.

Make 2 units, 4" × 4".

4 Repeat step 3, using two aqua gingham and two aqua floral half-square-triangle units to make two aqua Pinwheel blocks measuring 4" square.

5 Sew the Pinwheel blocks, six white side triangles, and two white corner triangles together into four units. Join the units. Sew two white corner triangles to the pieced row. Press. Trim the pinwheel border to 5½" × 20½", including the seam allowances.

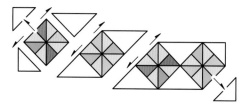

Make 1 border, 5½" × 20½".

ASSEMBLING THE QUILT TOP

Press the seam allowances as indicated by the arrows.

1 Stitch a white 1¾" × 5¾" rectangle to the left side of Apron block #1 and a white 1¾" × 5¾" rectangle right side of Apron block #2 as shown. Stitch a white 4¼" × 7¾" rectangle to the bottom of each apron unit.

2 Stitch the apron units to the Dress block.

3 Stitch the white 3¾" × 20½" rectangle to the top of the apron/dress unit and the white 3¼" × 20½" rectangle to the bottom.

4 Stitch the pinwheel border to the bottom. The quilt top should measure 20½" square.

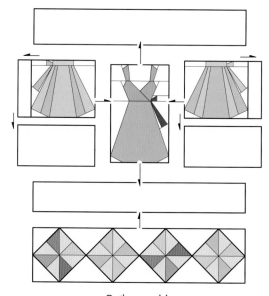

Quilt assembly

5 Using the pattern as a placement guide, transfer the clothesline and butterfly to the finished block. For the butterfly flight path, mark a swirling line referring to the diagram below for a suggestion.

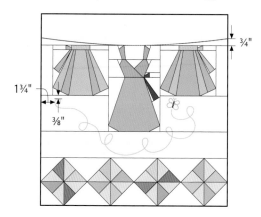

6 Using the backstitch and three strands of embroidery floss, stitch the clothesline with dark gray floss, the butterfly with dark pink floss, and the flight path and antennae with aqua floss.

Backstitch

FINISHING THE QUILT

1 Layer the quilt top, batting, and backing. Baste the layers together. Using a walking foot, quilt in the ditch around the aprons and dress. Quilt in the ditch around the pinwheels and along the seams inside the pinwheels.

2 Baste around the quilt, ¼" from the raw edge. Trim the backing and batting even with the edges of the quilt top.

3 Place the corner template from the sewing cottage pillow (pattern sheet 1) on one corner of the quilt. Trace the template, and then cut just inside the line. Repeat for the remaining corners.

4 Fold one end of the binding strip ¼" toward the wrong side. Place the folded end of the binding on the quilt back at the center bottom, right sides together with raw edges aligned. Pin in place.

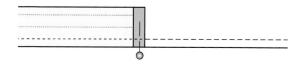

5 Stitch the binding to the back of the quilt. When you reach the starting point, overlap the folded end by ⅜". Trim the excess binding.

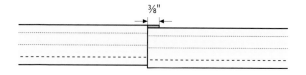

6 Fold the binding to the right side of the quilt, just covering the stitching. Pin in place. Press. Hand slip-stitch or machine stitch the binding to the front of the quilt.

Acknowledgments

Writing this book is a dream come true, and it wouldn't have been possible without the love and support of my family and friends.

I'd like to thank my husband, Jay, and my boys, Liam and Luc, for being supportive of my passion for sewing.

Thanks to my mom, Ann, for recognizing my need to create and teaching me how to sew. She is always supportive and proud of my endeavors. I love you!

Thanks to my dad, Miles, for giving me the courage to follow my dreams and passion and to take the leap to embark on a creative career. Love you, Dad!

Thanks to my dear grandmother, Carrie, who sewed the most beautiful things for me. Miss you!

Thanks to my best friend, Rose, who is like a sister to me, for being a sounding board and encouraging me to follow my dreams.

Thanks to the team at Martingale for helping me create the book I envisioned. A special thanks to Beth Bradley for believing in me and encouraging me to write this book. It has been such a pleasure to work with everyone!

About the Author

CHARISE RANDELL is a fashion designer who grew up sewing with her mother. She left her full-time job eight years ago to raise her boys and found quilting as a creative outlet. After joining online quilting bees, she discovered foundation paper piecing and was hooked.

Her style is inspired by vintage domestic arts and the beauty of simple craft. You can find her apparel, quilt, and accessory designs at ChariseCreates.blogspot.com.

- **Instagram:** ChariseCreates
- **Etsy:** etsy.com/shop/ChariseCreates?ref=si_shop
- **Craftsy:** craftsy.com/user/654996/pattern-store

What's your creative passion?

Find it at **ShopMartingale.com**

books • eBooks • ePatterns • blog • free projects
videos • tutorials • inspiration • giveaways

Create with Confidence